Hal Leonard Student Piano Library

Piano Lessons

T0034041

Book 5

FOREWORD

When music excites our interest and imagination, we eagerly put our hearts into learning it. The music in the **Hal Leonard Student Piano Library** encourages practice, progress, confidence, and best of all – success! Over 1,000 students and teachers in a nationwide test market responded with enthusiasm to the:

- variety of styles and moods
- natural rhythmic flow, singable melodies and lyrics
- "best ever" teacher accompaniments
- improvisations integrated throughout the **Lesson Books**
- orchestrated accompaniments included in audio and MIDI formats.

When new concepts have an immediate application to the music, the effort it takes to learn these skills seems worth it. Test market teachers and students were especially excited about the:

- "realistic" pacing that challenges without overwhelming
- clear and concise presentation of concepts that allows room for a teacher's individual approach
- uncluttered page layout that keeps the focus on the music.

The **Piano Practice Games** books are preparation activities to coordinate technique, concepts, and creativity with the actual music in **Piano Lessons**. In addition, the **Piano Theory Workbook** presents fun writing activities for review, and the **Piano Solos** series reinforces concepts with challenging performance repertoire.

The **Hal Leonard Student Piano Library** is the result of the efforts of many individuals. We extend our gratitude to all the teachers, students, and colleagues who shared their energy and creative input. May this method guide your learning as you bring this music to life.

Best wishes,

Barbara Kreader *Fred Kern* *Phillip Keveren*

Authors
**Barbara Kreader, Fred Kern,
Phillip Keveren**

Consultants
Mona Rejino, Tony Caramia,
Bruce Berr, Richard Rejino

Editor
Carol Klose

Illustrator
Fred Bell

To access audio, visit:
www.halleonard.com/mylibrary

ISBN 978-0-7935-9286-9

HAL•LEONARD®

Visit Hal Leonard Online at
www.halleonard.com

World headquarters, contact:
Hal Leonard
7777 West Bluemound Road
Milwaukee, WI 53213
Email: info@halleonard.com

In Europe, contact:
Hal Leonard Europe Limited
1 Red Place
London, W1K 6PL
Email: info@halleonardeurope.com

In Australia, contact:
Hal Leonard Australia Pty. Ltd.
4 Lentara Court
Cheltenham, Victoria, 3192 Australia
Email: info@halleonard.com.au

REVIEW OF BOOK FOUR

NOTE AND REST VALUES

eighth rest
fills the time of
one eighth note

eighth note triplet
fills the time of
one quarter note

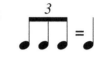

INTERVALS

Interval of a 7th

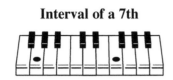

Interval of an Octave (8th)

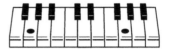

SCALES & PRIMARY TRIADS

C Major

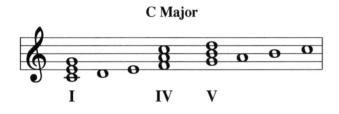

I   IV   V

A Minor

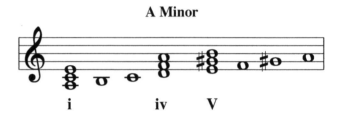

i   iv   V

G Major

I   IV   V

E Minor

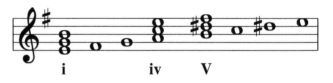

i   iv   V

TIME SIGNATURES

$\frac{3}{8}$ $\left(\begin{array}{c}\mathbf{3}\\\mathbf{♪}\end{array}\right)$ three beats fill every measure
eighth note gets one beat

common time C $\left(\begin{array}{c}\mathbf{4}\\\mathbf{♩}\end{array}\right)$ another name for $\frac{4}{4}$
has the feeling of four beats
per measure

$\frac{6}{8}$ $\left(\begin{array}{c}\mathbf{6}\\\mathbf{♪}\end{array}\right)$ six beats fill every measure
eighth note gets one beat

cut time ¢ $\left(\begin{array}{c}\mathbf{2}\\\mathbf{♩}\end{array}\right)$ two beats fill the measure
half note gets one beat

MUSICAL TERMS

accidentals – ♯, ♭, ♮ added to a piece outside the key signature

allegretto – slightly slower than *allegro*

con moto – with motion

diminuendo (dim.) – gradually softer

dominant – 5th tone of the scale (V)

etude – exercise or study

giocoso – with humor

moderato – medium tempo

poco – a little; slightly

presto – very fast

sub-dominant – 4th tone of the scale (IV)

tenuto – give the note extra emphasis, holding it for its full value

tonic – 1st tone of the scale (I)

vivace – lively

CONTENTS

PLAYING IN F MAJOR & D MINOR

* Students can check pieces as they play them.

Windmill

UNIT 1

Wistfully (♩. = 86)

Phillip Keveren

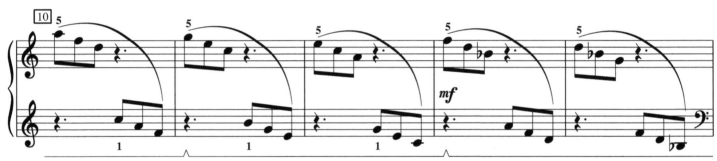

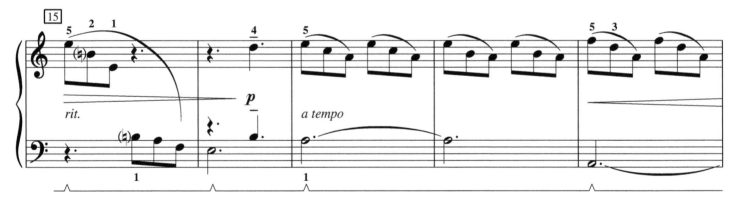

molto - much

The Bear

Vladimir Rebikoff
(1866-1920)

Andante pesante* (♩=90)

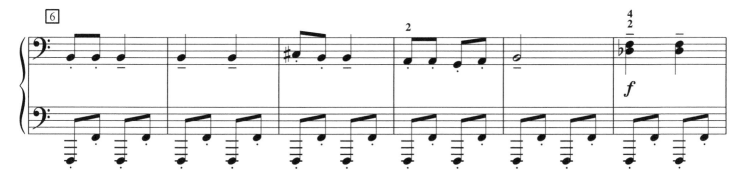

*pesante - heavy

Arabesque

Fredrich Burgmüller
(1806-1874)
Op. 100

Allegro scherzando* (♩=110)

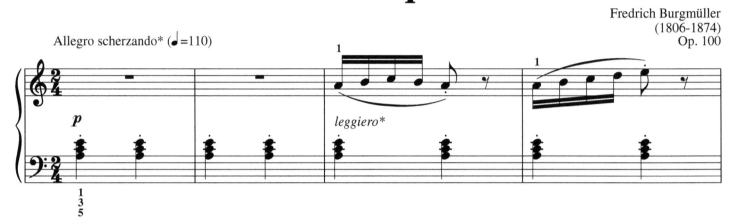

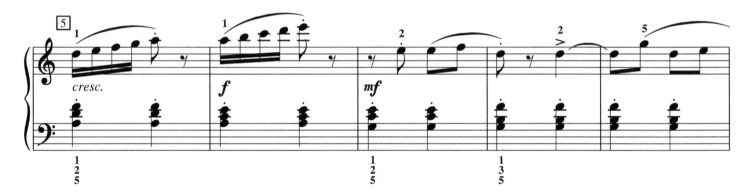

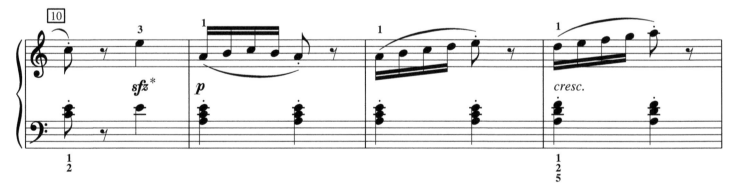

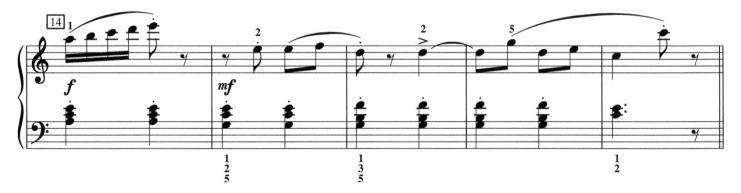

* *scherzando* - playfully   * *leggiero* - lightly   * **sfz** *sforzando* - sudden strong accent

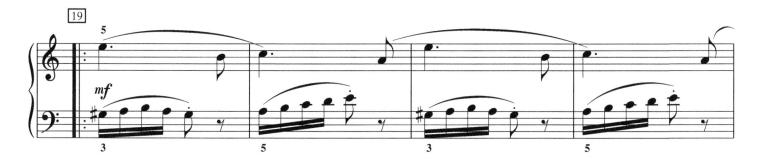

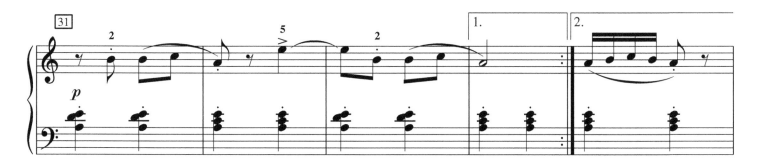

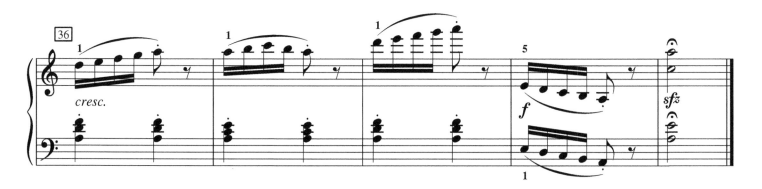

F Major Scale Pattern

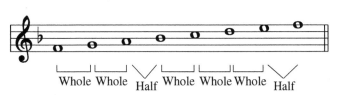

Whole   Whole   Half   Whole   Whole   Whole   Half

The Primary Triads in **F Major** are:

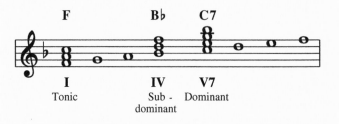

I	IV	V7
Tonic	Sub-dominant	Dominant

Moving On Up

Key of F Major
Key signature: *one flat, B♭*

Moderato
Scale

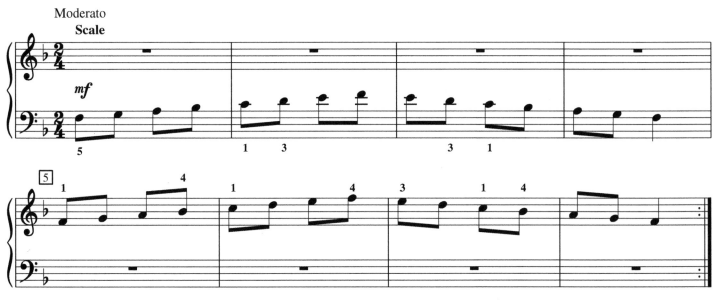

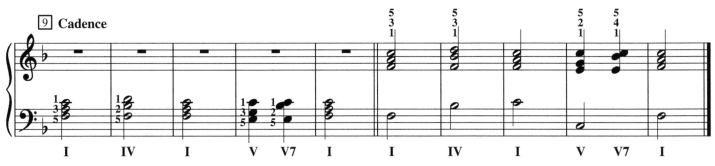

⑨ **Cadence**

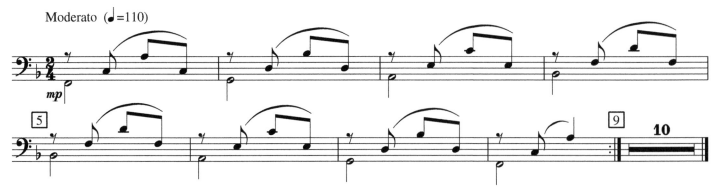

I   IV   I   V   V7   I   I   IV   I   V   V7   I

Accompaniment (Student plays one octave higher than written.)

Moderato (♩=110)

mp

⑤ ⑨ **10**

Extra for Experts
Turn to page 52 to play scales and cadences in **C Major** and **G Major**.

D Minor Scale Patterns
Natural Minor

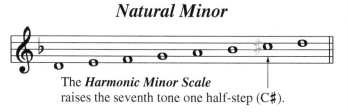

The ***Harmonic Minor Scale***
raises the seventh tone one half-step (C♯).

The Primary Triads in **D Minor** are:

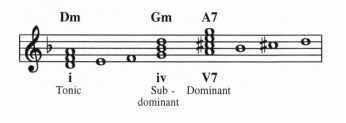

Dm	**Gm**	**A7**
i	**iv**	**V7**
Tonic	Sub- dominant	Dominant

Moving On Up

Key of D Minor
Key signature: *one flat, B♭*

First, play the ***Natural Minor Scale*** with the B♭ only.
On the repeat, play the ***Harmonic Minor Scale*** with the raised 7th (C♯).

Accompaniment (Student plays two octaves higher than written.)

First, play the natural form with the B♭ only. On the repeat, play the harmonic form with the raised 7th (C♯).

Extra for Experts
Turn to page 53 to play scales and cadences in **A Minor** and **E Minor.**

My Own Song
in F Major & D Minor

Improvising with Motives and Sequences

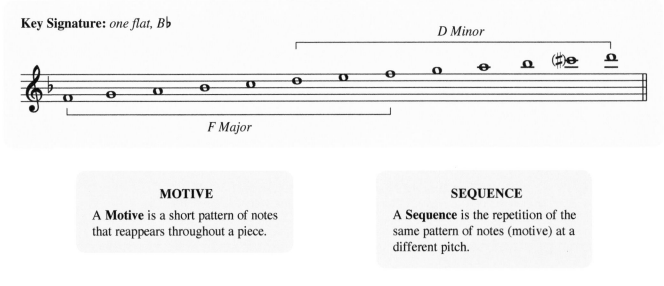

Key Signature: *one flat, B♭*

D Minor

F Major

MOTIVE

A **Motive** is a short pattern of notes that reappears throughout a piece.

SEQUENCE

A **Sequence** is the repetition of the same pattern of notes (motive) at a different pitch.

Shape your improvisation using **motives** and **sequences**.

1. Play the following one-measure **motive**.
    Improvise by playing various **sequences** of this motive using notes from the F Major Scale.

Accompaniment

Moderato (♩=100)

Repeat as necessary | *Last time*

2. Play the following one-measure **motive**.
    Improvise by playing various **sequences** of this motive using notes from the D Harmonic Minor Scale.

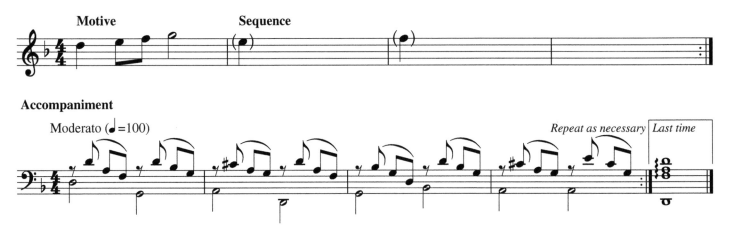

Accompaniment

Moderato (♩=100)

Repeat as necessary | *Last time*

Extra for Experts

As you listen to the accompaniment in F Major, create your own motive and improvise various sequences.
Do the same in D Minor.

SIXTEENTH REST

A **Sixteenth Rest** fills the time of one sixteenth note.

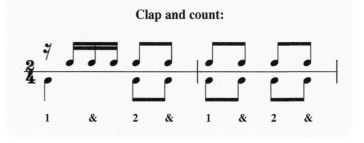
Spinning A Yarn

Playfully (♩=94)

Phillip Keveren

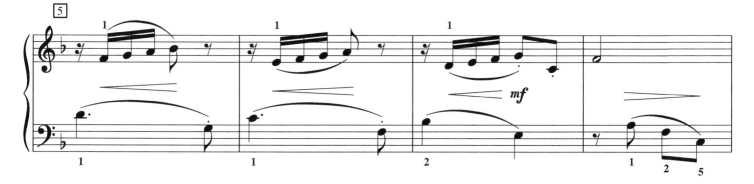

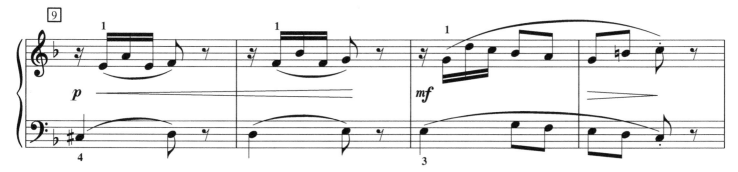

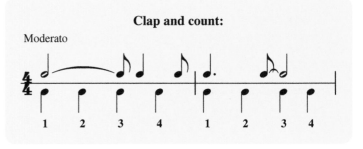

Wade In The Water

Spiritual
Arranged by Fred Kern

Moderato (♩=140)

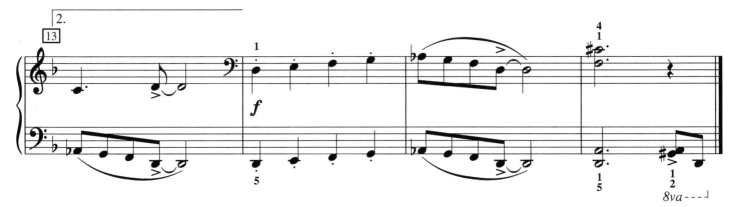

12

SIXTEENTH NOTE PATTERNS

Clap and count:

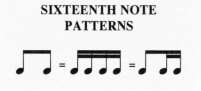

Simple Gifts

American
Arranged by Barbara Kreader

Flowing (♪=104)

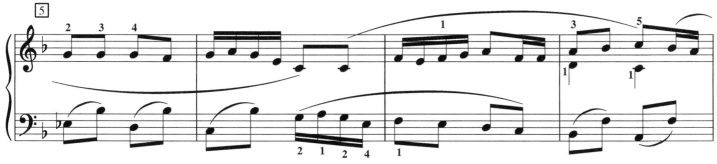

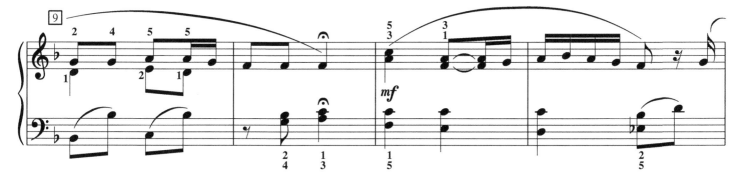

Innocence

Fredrich Burgmüller
(1806-1874)
Op. 100

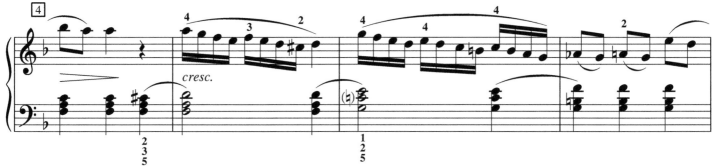

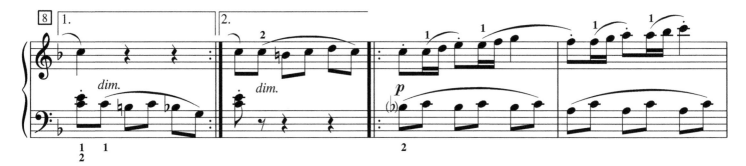

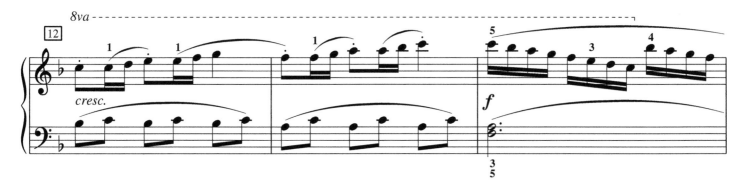

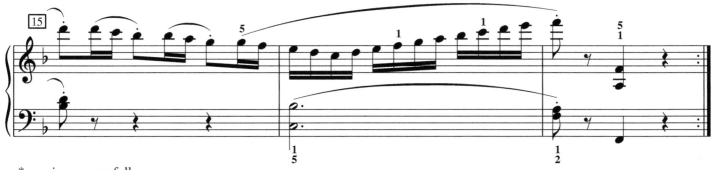

* *grazioso* - gracefully

A Minor Contribution

Moderate Swing (♪♪ = ♪ ♪) (♩ =120)

Bill Boyd

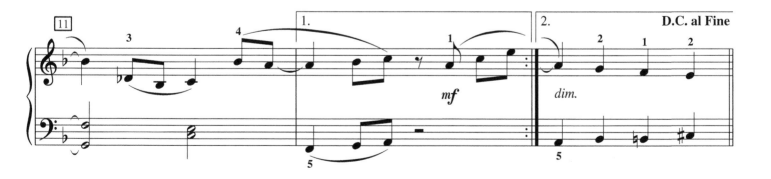

Chord Qualities

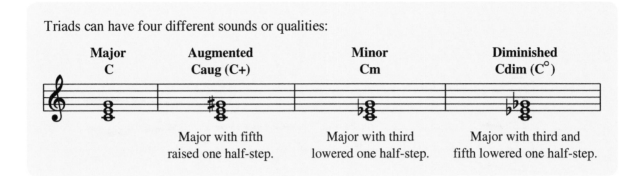

Triads can have four different sounds or qualities:

Major	Augmented	Minor	Diminished
C	Caug (C+)	Cm	Cdim (C°)
	Major with fifth raised one half-step.	Major with third lowered one half-step.	Major with third and fifth lowered one half-step.

Cartoon Villain

Phillip Keveren

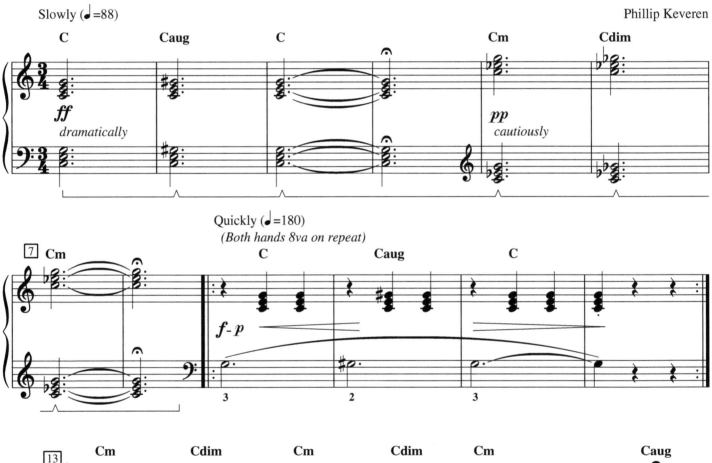

Slowly (♩=88)

Quickly (♩=180)
(Both hands 8va on repeat)

* accel. (accelerando) - becoming faster

Extra for Experts
Transpose *Cartoon Villain* to **G Major** and **F Major**.

Chords of the Key

PRIMARY TRIADS

Chords built on the 1st, 4th, and 5th tones of the major scale are called **Primary Triads**.

These triads are **major** and use *upper case* Roman Numerals **I - IV - V**.

SECONDARY TRIADS

Chords built on the 2nd, 3rd, and 6th tones of the major scale are called **Secondary Triads**.

These triads are **minor** and use *lower case* Roman Numerals **ii - iii - vi**.

On The Rise

The chord built on the 7th tone of the major scale is diminished (**vii°**).

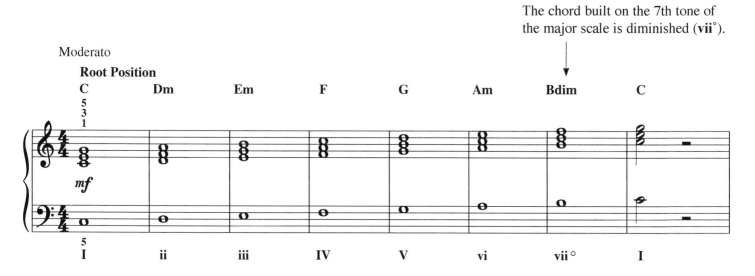

Open Position - one or more chord tones moved an octave higher or lower.
In these open chords, the 3rd is moved an octave higher.

Accompaniment

Moderato (♩=110)

Extra for Experts
Turn to pages 54-55 to play Chords of the Key in **G Major** and **F Major** in root and open positions.

17

Curtain Call

Phillip Keveren

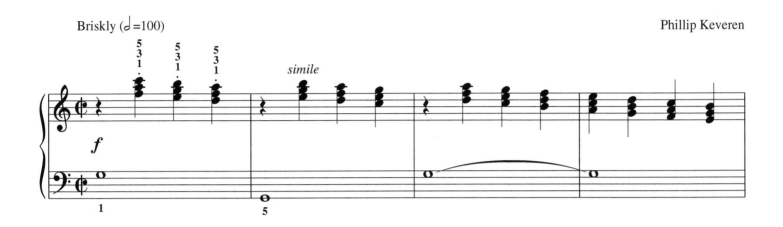

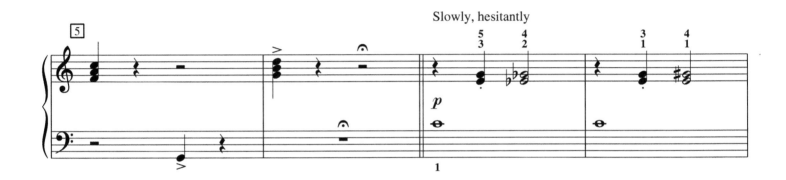

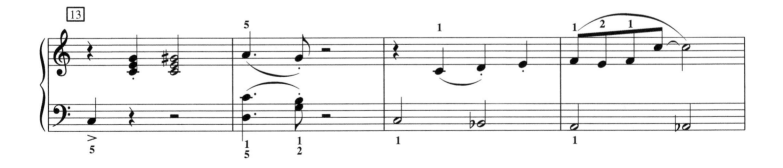

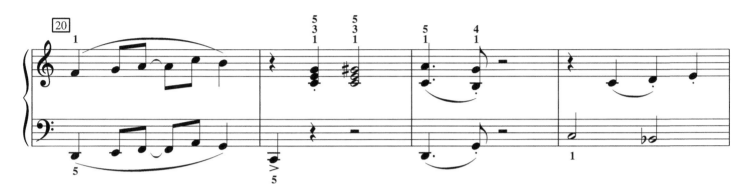

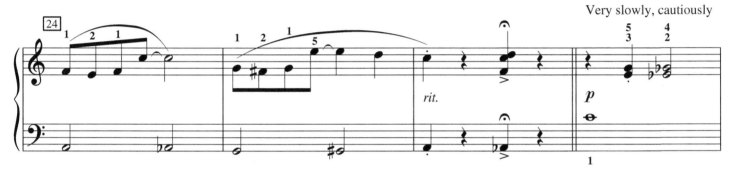

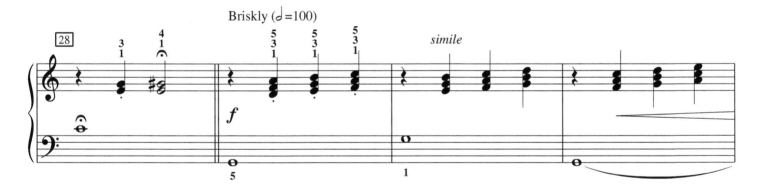

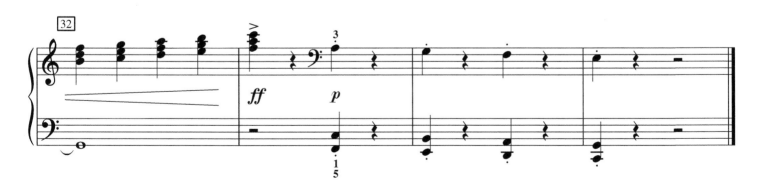

Open Position Triads in F Major:

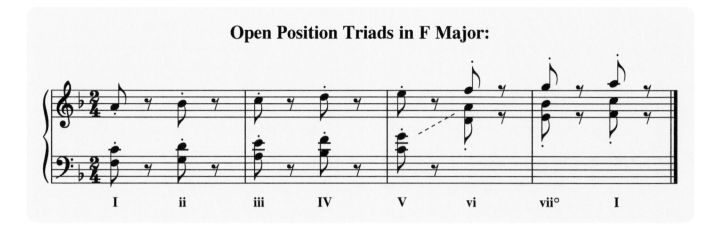

I   ii   iii   IV   V   vi   vii°   I

The Clown

Vladimir Rebikov
(1866 - 1920)

Allegretto (♩=96)

D Major Scale Pattern

The Primary Triads in **D Major** are:

D	G	A7
I	IV	V7
Tonic	Sub-dominant	Dominant

Moving On Up

Key of D Major
Key signature: *two sharps, F♯ C♯*

Moderato

Scale

(music notation, measures 1–8)

9 Cadence

I IV I V V7 I I IV I V V7 I

Accompaniment (Student plays two octaves higher than written.)

Moderato (♩=110)

Extra for Experts
Turn to page 52 to play the scale and cadence in **F Major.**

B Minor Scale Patterns
Natural Minor

The *Harmonic Minor Scale*
raises the 7th tone one half-step (A♯).

The Primary Triads in **B Minor** are:

Bm	Em	F♯7
i	iv	V7
Tonic	Sub - dominant	Dominant

Moving On Up

Key of B Minor
Key signature: *two sharps, F♯ C♯*

First, play the *Natural Minor Scale* with the F♯, C♯ only.
On the repeat, play the *Harmonic Minor Scale* with the raised 7th (A♯).

Moderato

Accompaniment (Student plays two octaves higher than written.)

First, play the natural form with the F♯, C♯ only. On the repeat, play the harmonic form with the raised 7th (A♯).

Moderato (♩=110)

Extra for Experts
Turn to page 53 to play the scale and cadence in **D Minor.**

My Own Song
in D Major & B Minor

Improvising Question and Answer Phrases

Key Signature: *two sharps, F♯ C♯*

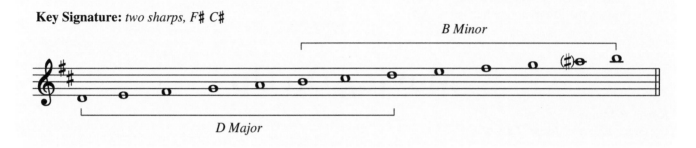

Shape your improvisation using **question** and **answer** phrases.

1. Play the following two-measure **question** phrase. Improvise various **answers** using notes from the D Major Scale.
   • *Parallel answers* begin with the same pitches and include an almost identical ending.
   • *Contrasting answers* include musical material different from the question.

Accompaniment

1. Play the following two-measure **question** phrase.
   Improvise various **answers** using notes from the B Harmonic Minor Scale.

Accompaniment

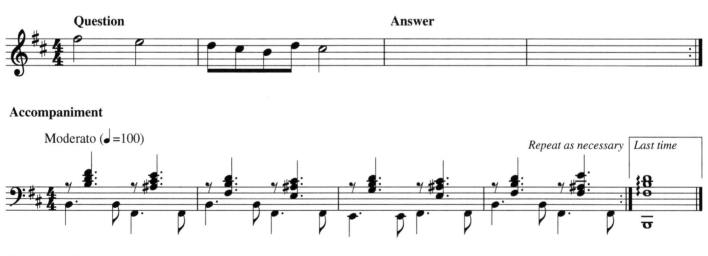

Extra for Experts
As you listen to the accompaniment in D Major, create your own question and improvise various answers.
Do the same in B Minor.

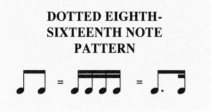

DOTTED EIGHTH-SIXTEENTH NOTE PATTERN

Clap and count:

A Whispered Promise

Slowly, with tenderness (♩=76)

Phillip Keveren

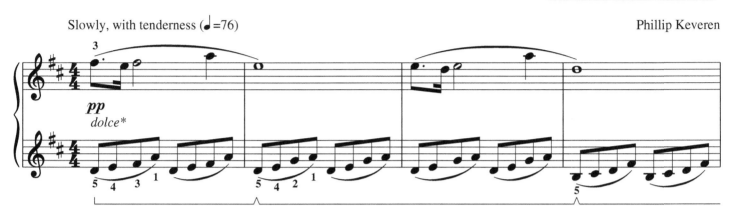

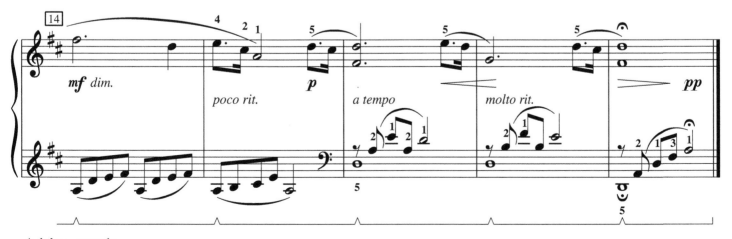

* *dolce* - sweetly

The Kind Cuckoo

Les Coucous Benevoles

François Couperin
(1668-1733)

Moderato (♩=90)

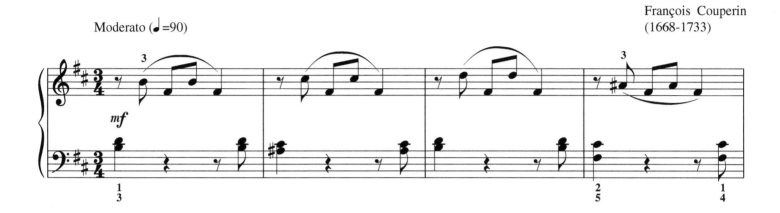

GRACE NOTE

An ornamental note, usually
played quickly, before the beat.

Nothing Could Be Finer Than Minor

Slowly (Four heavy beats to the measure) (♩=90)

Bill Boyd

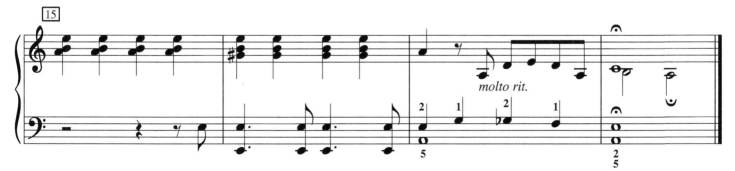

Fantasia

Georg Philipp Telemann
(1681-1767)

Vivace (♩=100)

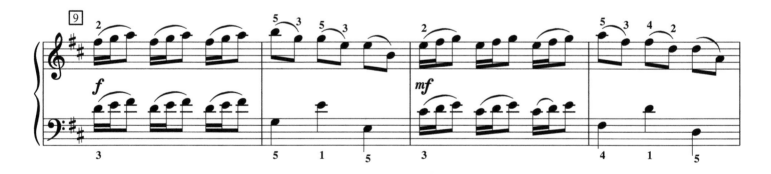

28

Scherzino

Samuel Maykapar
(1867-1938)

Allegro scherzando (♪=176)

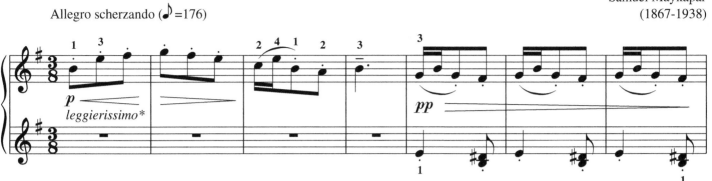

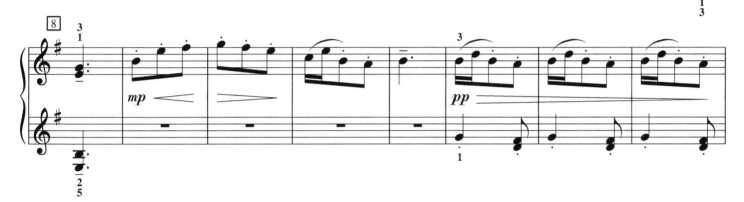

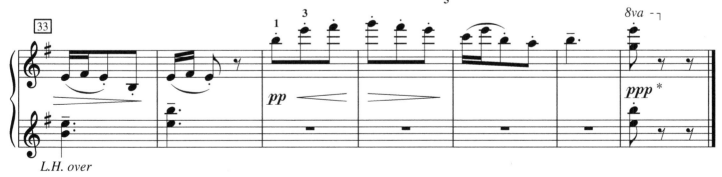

L.H. over

* *leggierissimo* - very lightly * ***ppp*** - very, very softly

29

Chords of the Key

Root, First, and Second Inversions

A triad can have **three** positions:

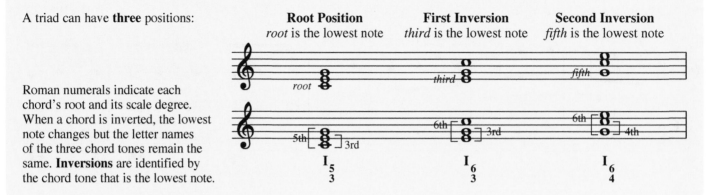

Roman numerals indicate each chord's root and its scale degree. When a chord is inverted, the lowest note changes but the letter names of the three chord tones remain the same. **Inversions** are identified by the chord tone that is the lowest note.

Chords of the Key in First Inversion

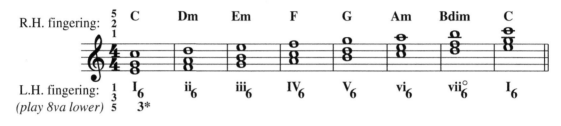

Bouncing Back

Tempo de dribble ($\downarrow$=170)

Phillip Keveren

* In **first inversion** chords, the number 3 indicating the interval of a 3rd is generally omitted, and the chord symbol is often abbreviated: I_6, ii_6, etc.

Chords of the Key in Second Inversion

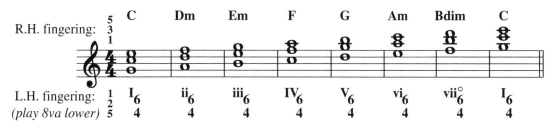

Michael, Row The Boat Ashore

American
Arranged by Fred Kern

Simply and smoothly (♩=96)

Extra for Experts
Turn to page 54 to play Chords of the Key in **G Major**, **F Major**, and **D Major** in first and second inversions.

Romance In B Minor

Andante espressivo * (♩ = 112)

Phillip Keveren

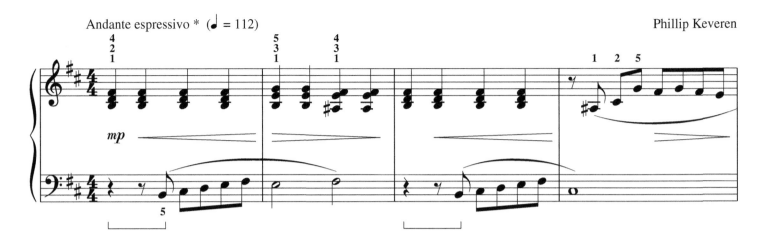

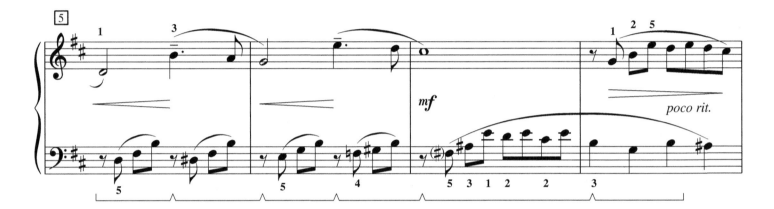

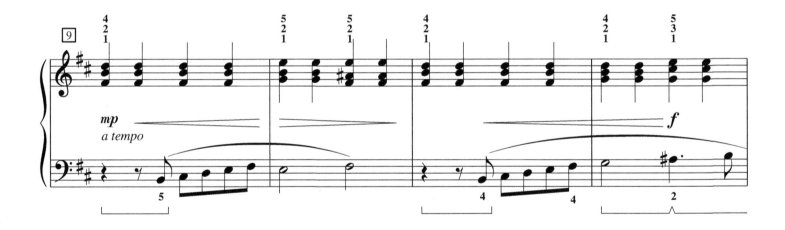

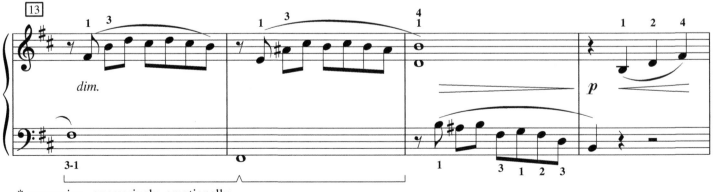

espressivo - expressively, emotionally

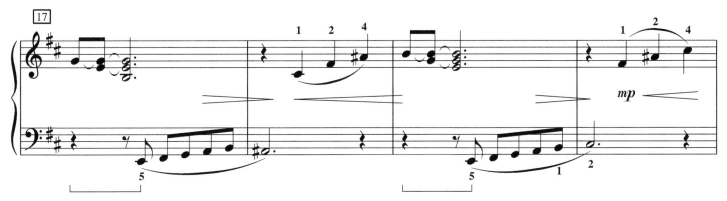

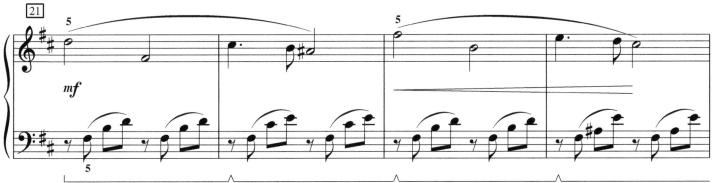

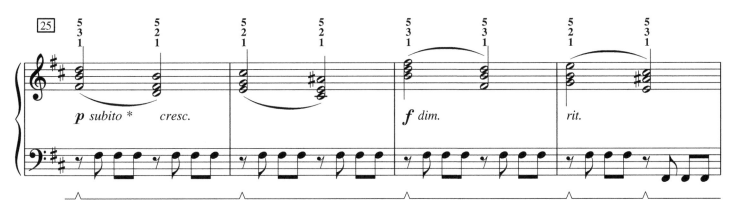

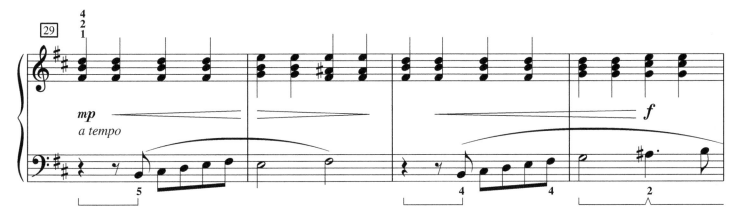

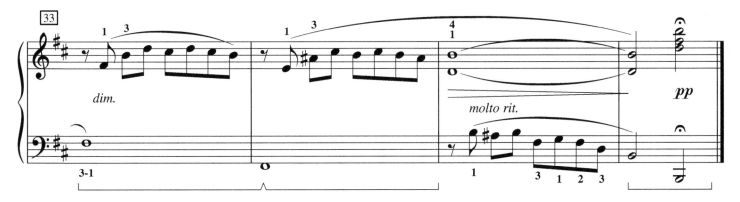

subito - suddenly

33

Bethena

Scott Joplin
(1868-1917)
Arranged by Fred Kern

Waltz tempo (♩=108)

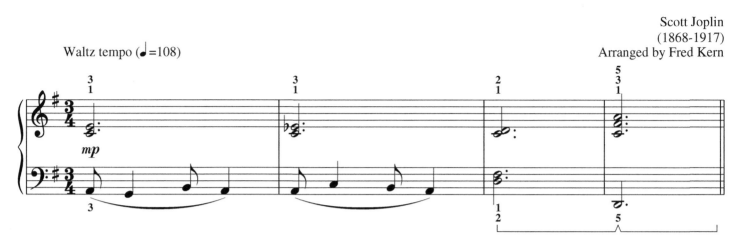

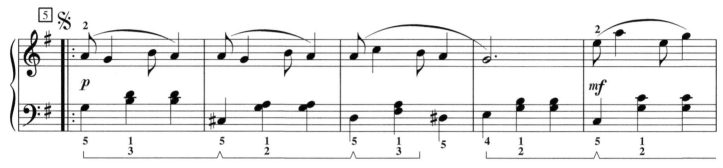

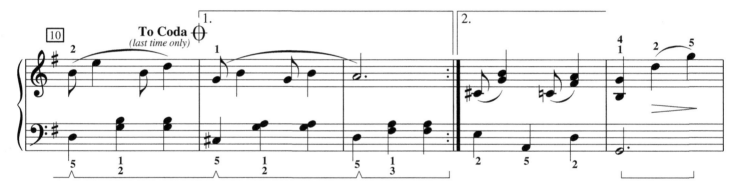

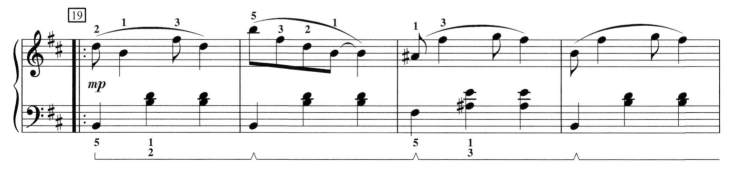

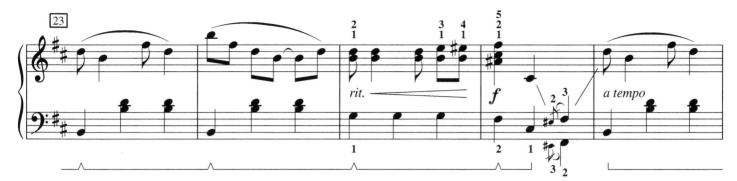

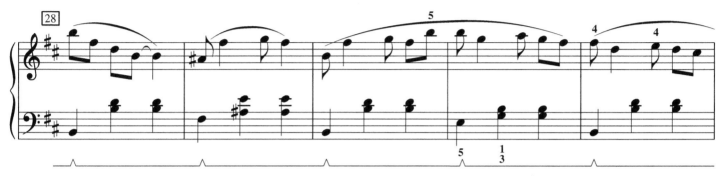

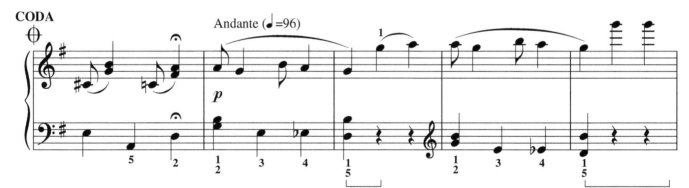

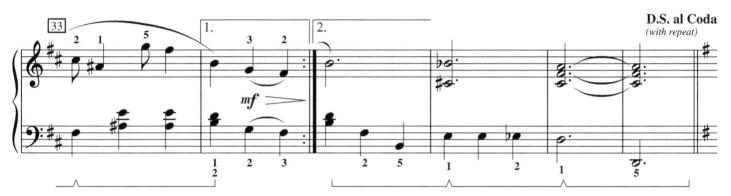

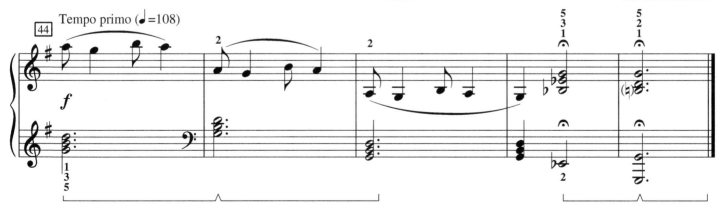

B♭ Major Scale Pattern

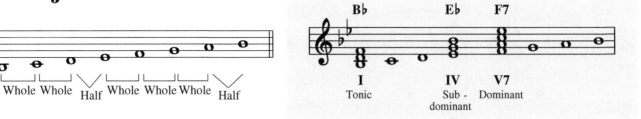

Whole Whole Half Whole Whole Whole Half

The Primary Triads in **B♭ Major** are:

B♭   E♭   F7

I   IV   V7

Tonic   Sub -   Dominant
dominant

Moving On Up

Key of B♭ Major
Key signature: *two flats, B♭ E♭*

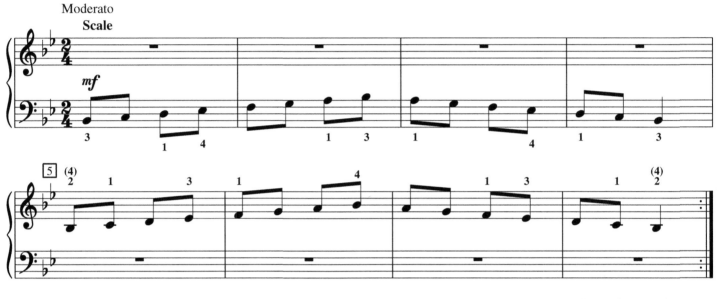

Moderato
Scale

Cadence

I   IV   I   V   V7   I   I   IV   I   V   V7   I

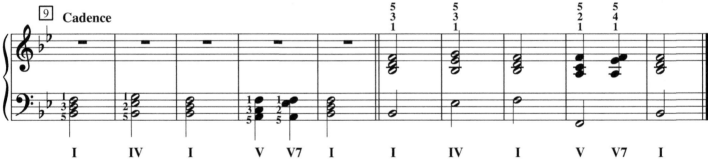

Accompaniment (Student plays two octaves higher than written.)

Moderato (♩=110)

Extra for Experts
Turn to page 52 to play the scale and cadence in **D Major.**

G Minor Scale Patterns
Natural Minor

The *Harmonic Minor Scale*
raises the seventh tone one half-step (F♯).

The Primary Triads in **G Minor** are:

Gm	Cm	D7
i	**iv**	**V7**
Tonic	Sub-dominant	Dominant

Moving On Up

Key of G Minor
Key signature: *two flats, B♭ E♭*

First, play the *Natural Minor Scale* with the B♭, E♭ only.
On the repeat, play the *Harmonic Minor Scale* with the raised 7th (F♯).

Moderato

Accompaniment (Student plays one octave higher than written.)

First, play the natural form with the B♭, E♭ only. On the repeat, play the harmonic form with the raised 7th (F♯).

Moderato (♩=110)

Extra for Experts
Turn to page 53 to play the scale and cadence in **B Minor**.

My Own Song
in B♭ Major & G Minor
Improvising in A B A Form

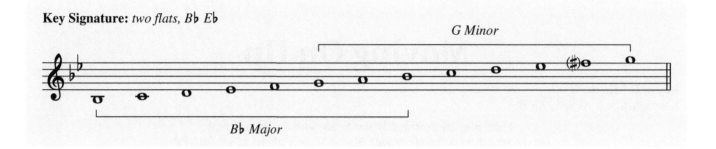

Key Signature: *two flats, B♭ E♭*

Shape your improvisation using **A B A form**.

1. To create the **A section**, play the following two-measure question phrase.
   Improvise various answers (*parallel* or *contrasting*), using notes from the B♭ Major Scale.

2. To create the **B section**, play the following motive. Improvise various sequences using notes from the
   G Harmonic Minor Scale.

Return to the **A section** in B♭ Major.

Accompaniment

Moderato (♩=100)

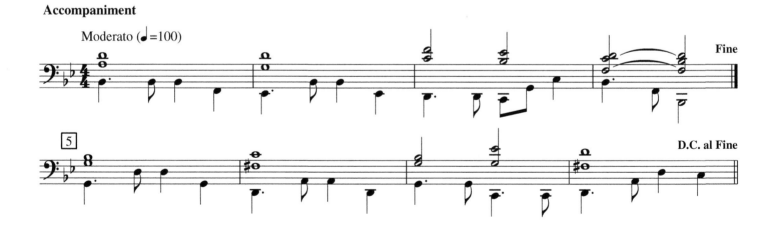

Allegro

Wolfgang Amadeus Mozart
(1756 - 1791)

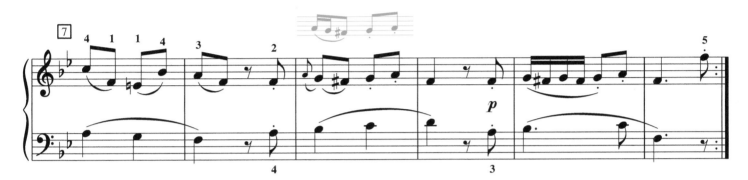

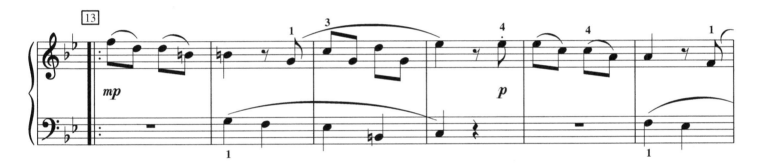

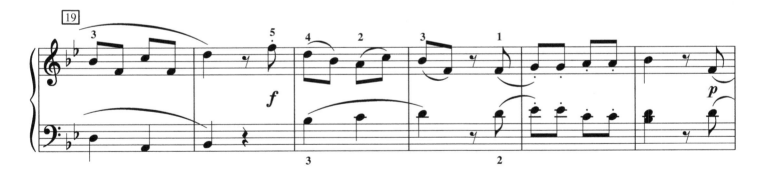

Extra for Experts
Turn to page 52 to play the scale and cadence in **B♭ Major.**

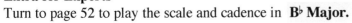

39

Menuet In G Minor

From the *Notebook for
Anna Magdalena Bach*

Allegro moderato (♩=100)

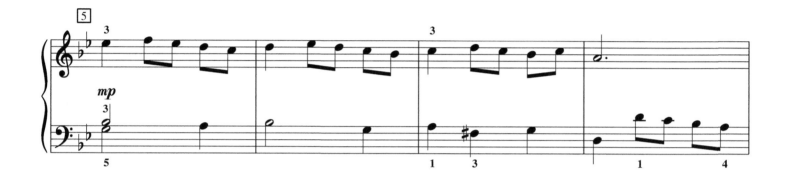

Extra for Experts

Turn to page 53 to play the scale and cadence in **G Minor.**

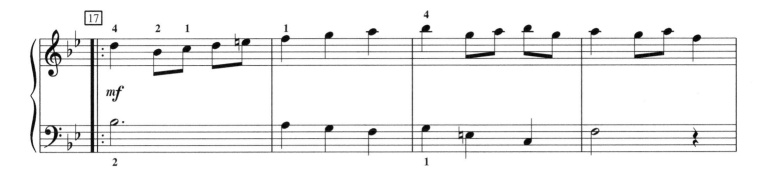

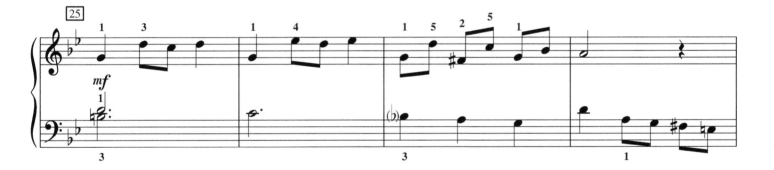

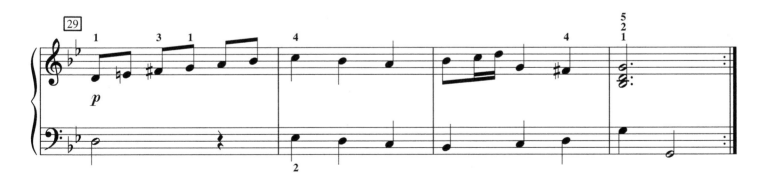

41

CHROMATIC SCALES

A **Chromatic Scale** is formed by playing half steps up and down the keyboard.

Finger 3 plays all black keys.

Fingers 1 and 2 play all white keys.

Left Hand   Right Hand

Inspector Hound Returns

Sneaky (♩=128)

Phillip Keveren

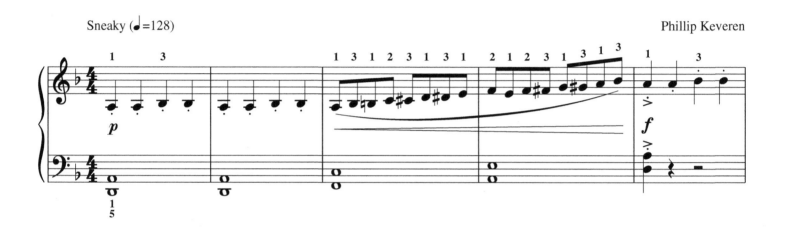

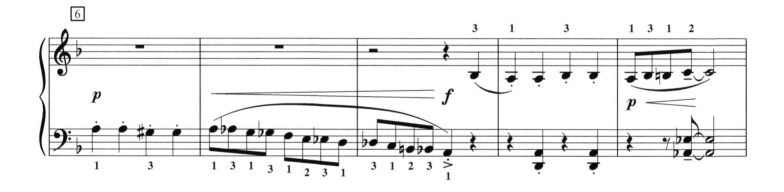

Prelude

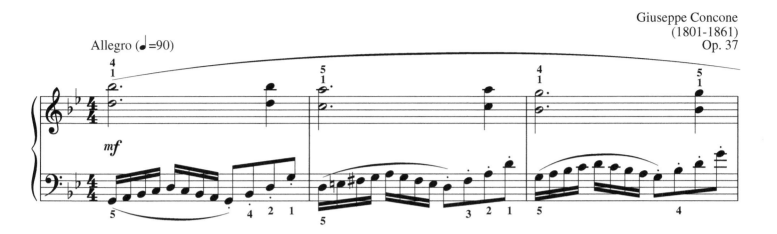

Giuseppe Concone
(1801-1861)
Op. 37

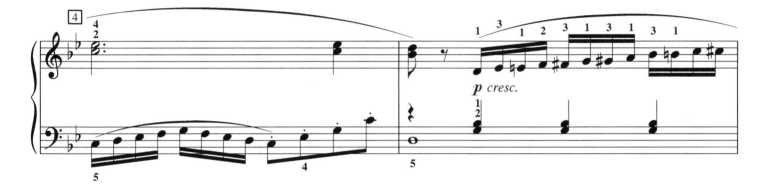

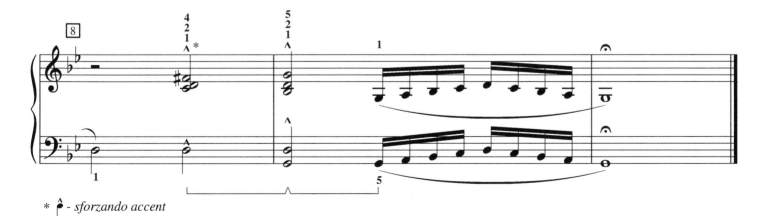

* $\hat{p}$ - *sforzando accent*

Wanderer's Song

Hugo Reinhold
(1854-1935)

Allegretto (♩=96)

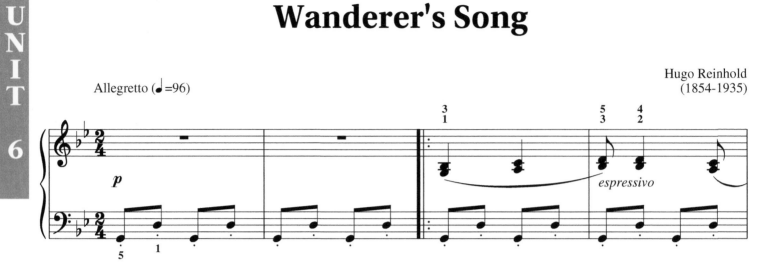

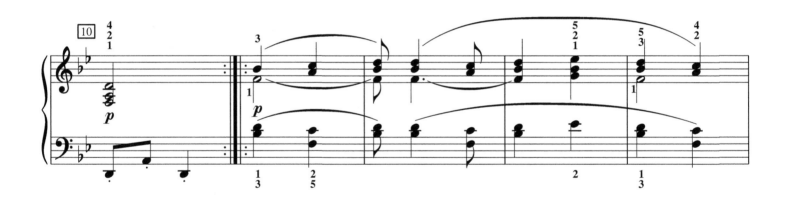

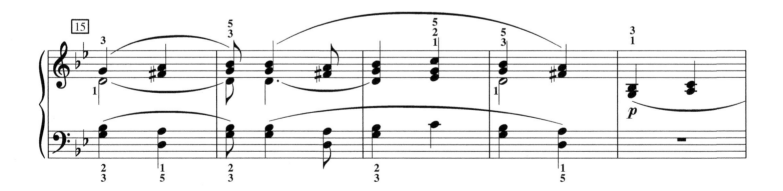

Extra for Experts

Turn to page 54 to play Chords of the Key in **B♭ Major,** in root, first, and second inversion.

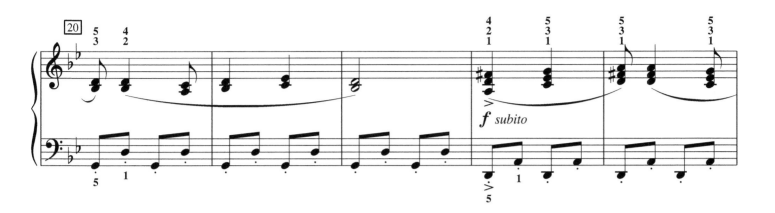

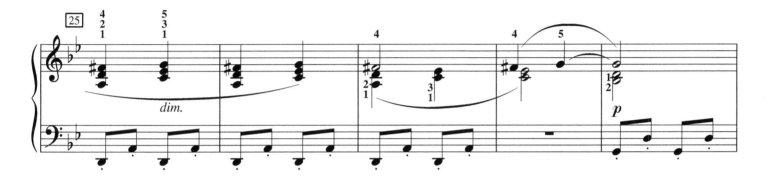

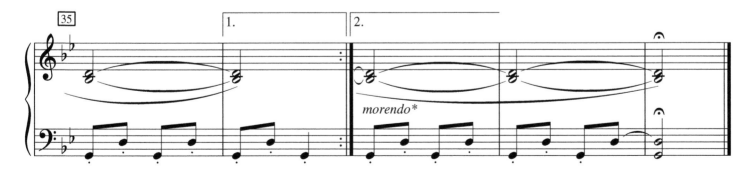

* *morendo* - "dying;" fading away

Everybody's Blues

Swing (♩♩ = ♩³♪) (♩=120)

Bill Boyd

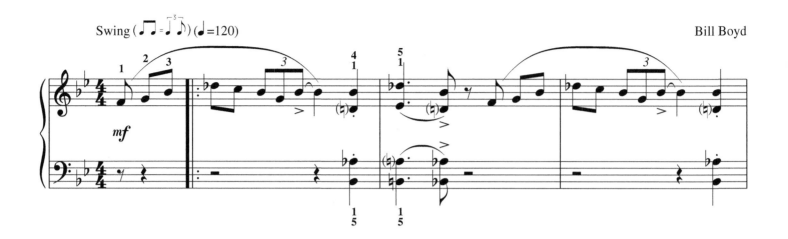

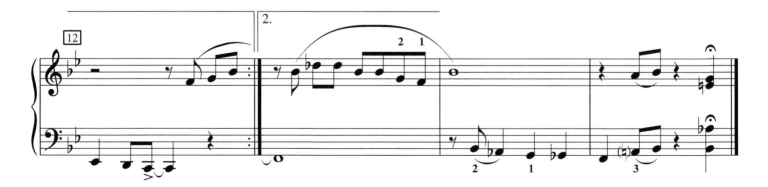

German Dance

Ludwig van Beethoven
(1770-1827)

Moderato (♩=125)

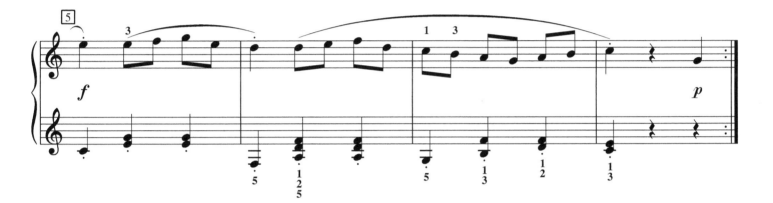

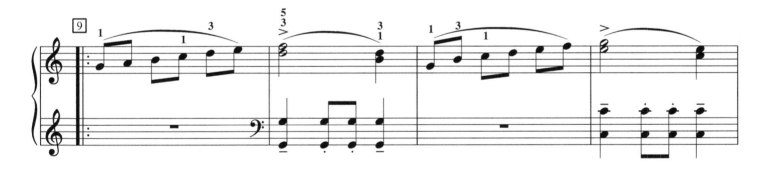

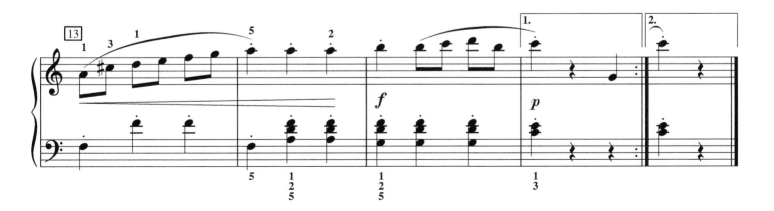

Canon In D

Johann Pachelbel
(1653-1706)
Arranged by Fred Kern

Andante (♩=84)

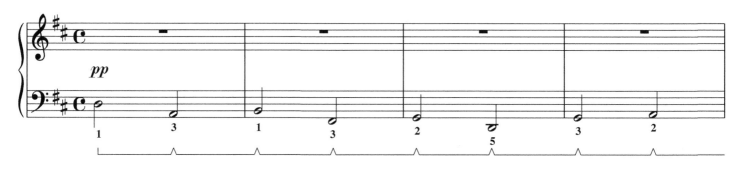

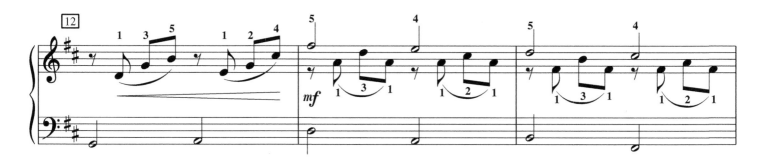

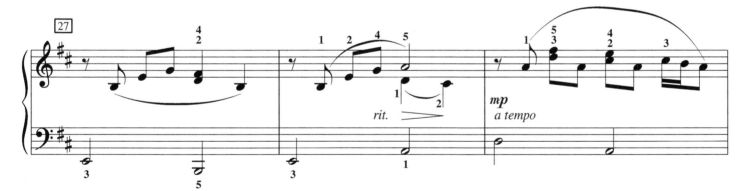

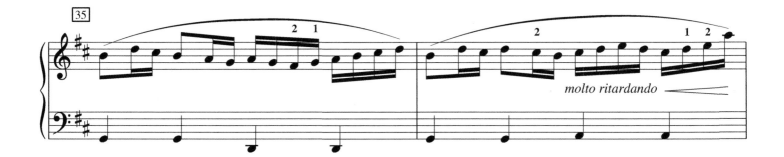

* *allargando* - broad *ritard*

GLOSSARY

Accelerando	Becoming faster.	*Molto*	Very.
Allargando	Broad *ritard.*	**Motive**	A short pattern of notes that reappears throughout a piece.
Arabesque	A fanciful piano piece; "Arabian."	*Morendo*	"Dying;" fading away.
Augmented triad	A Major triad with the fifth raised one half-step.	**Open position**	Chord with one or more tones moved an octave higher or lower.
Canon	A melody that is repeated exactly by a different voice.	**Parallel answer**	A phrase that repeats its question note for note.
Chromatic	Moving by half-steps.	*Pesante*	Heavily.
Close position	Chord tones played as close together as possible, usually within an octave.	**Pitch**	The highness or lowness of a tone.
Contrasting answer	A phrase that begins the same as the question but varies the ending.	*Poco a poco*	Little by little.
Diminished triad	A Minor triad with the fifth lowered one half-step.	*Portato*	Half *staccato*; halfway between *staccato* and *legato*.
Dolce	Sweetly.	*Portamento*	A smooth glide from one note to another.
Espressivo	Expressively, emotionally.	**Primary triad**	Triad built on the 1st, 4th, or 5th tone of any scale.
Free-style answer	A phrase that is completely different from its question.	*Scherzando*	Playfully.
Grace note	An ornamental note, usually played quickly, before the beat.	**Secondary triad**	Triad built on the 2nd, 3rd, or 6th tone of any scale.
Grazioso	Gracefully.	**Sequence**	Repetition of the same pattern of notes at a different pitch.
Inversion	A chord in which the bass note is not the root.	*Sforzando* *sfz*	A sudden strong accent.
Key	The tonal center based on the tonic note of the scale.	*Sforzando accent*	
Leggiero	Lightly.	*Subito*	Suddenly.
Marcato	Stressed, accented note.	*Tempo primo*	Return to first tempo.
Menuet (Minuet)	A French dance from the mid-1600's in slow $\frac{3}{4}$ time.		

MASTER COMPOSERS IN PIANO LESSONS BOOK FIVE

Baroque
1600

François Couperin (1668-1733)
French baroque composer.

Johann Pachelbel (1653-1706)
German baroque composer and organist.
Although he wrote several pieces for organ, his most popular composition is the *Canon in D* for strings.

Georg Philipp Telemann (1681-1767)
German baroque and pre-classical composer. He wrote much sacred music as well as many operas, concertos, and sonatas.

Classical
1750

Wolfgang Amadeus Mozart (1756-1791)
Austrian classical composer.
He began writing music at the age of five.

Ludwig van Beethoven (1770-1827)
German composer and pianist whose style bridged the classical and romantic eras. Among his many enduring works are 9 symphonies, 32 piano sonatas, and 5 piano concertos. During his final years, he wrote many compositions despite being completely deaf.

Giuseppe Concone (1801-1861)
Italian classical composer.

Fredrich Burgmüller (1806-1874)
German romantic composer who mainly composed study pieces for piano.

Romantic
1820

Hugo Reinhold (1854-1935)
German romantic composer.

Vladimir Rebikov (1866-1920)
Russian contemporary composer.

Scott Joplin (1868-1917)
African-American popular composer, known as the "King of Ragtime."

Samuel Maykapar (1867-1938)
Russian contemporary composer.

CONTEMPORARY
1900

Major Scales and Cadences

Play each scale:
- *Hands separately.*
- *Contrary Motion* – start on the same tonic note and play in opposite directions.
- *Parallel Motion* – play as written.

C Major Scale

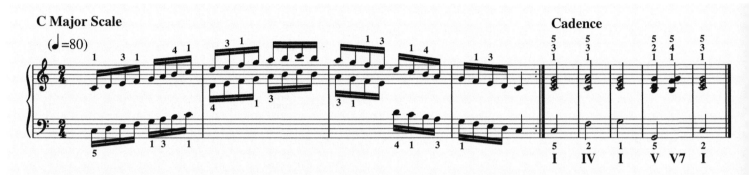

G Major Scale

F Major Scale

D Major Scale

B♭ Major Scale

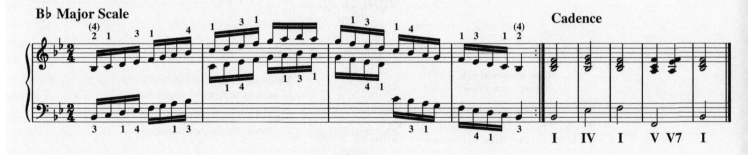

Minor Scales and Cadences

Play each **Harmonic Minor Scale:**
- *Hands separately.*
- *Contrary Motion* – start on the same tonic note and play in opposite directions.
- *Parallel Motion* – play as written.

Chords of the Key
Root Position & Inversions

		5	5	5
R.H.		3	2	3
		1	1	1
		Root	*1st Inversion*	*2nd Inversion*
L.H.		1	1	1
		3	3	2
		5	5	5

Observe the following chord fingering for each hand:

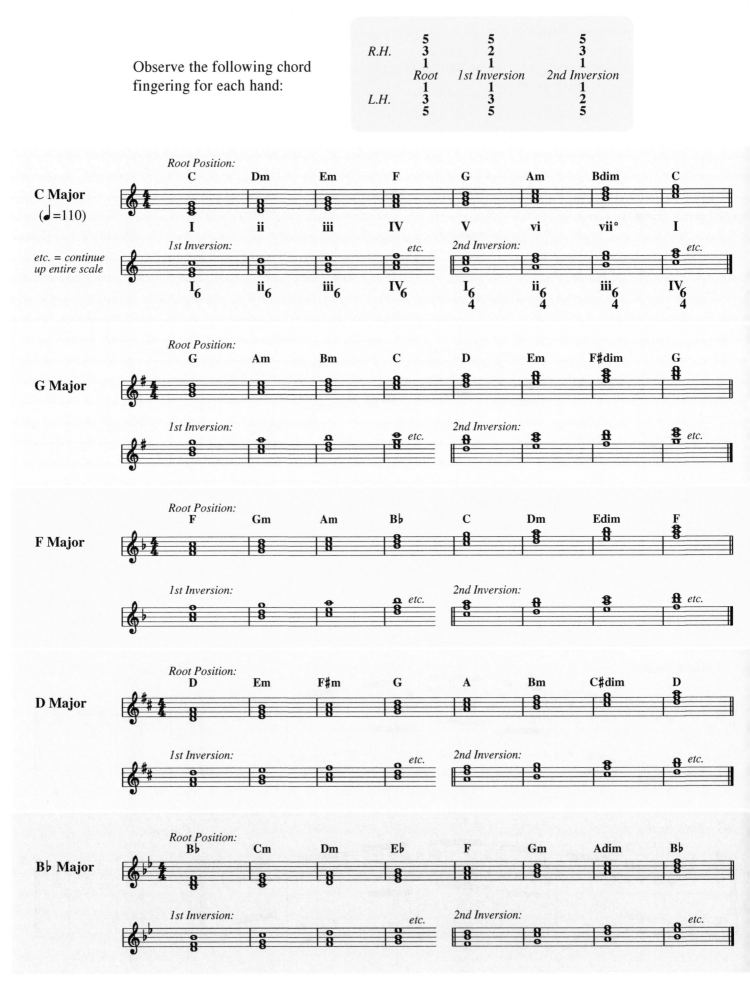

etc. = continue up entire scale

54

Chords of the Key
Open Position

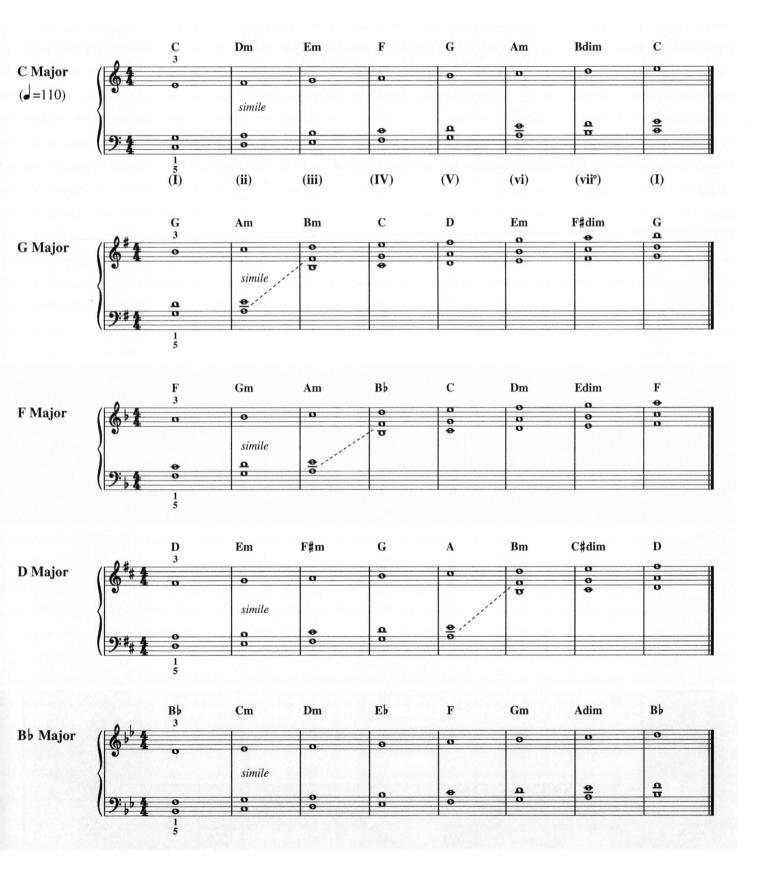

HAS SUCCESSFULLY COMPLETED
HAL LEONARD PIANO LESSONS,
BOOK FIVE.

TEACHER   DATE

HAL•LEONARD®